To our parents,
Who inspired us to explore
and experience the world around us.

Sorella Books
P.O. Box 454
Plantsville, Connecticut 06479

www.sorellabooks.com

Printed in China

ISBN 0-9767351-0-5

Pack Your Bags... Go U.S.A.

Written by Kimberley Weaver & Allyson Murphy

Illustrated by Maria K. Holdren

AL
Montgomery ★

ALABAMA
The Yellowhammer State

Aaron goes to Alabama. What does he do?

State Flag

Camellia

Yellowhammer

Explores the sites in Birmingham

Alexandra goes to Alaska. What does she see?

Mount McKinley

State Flag

Forget-Me-Not

Willow Ptarmigan

ARIZONA
The Grand Canyon State

AZ

Phoenix ★

Abby goes to Arizona. What does she see?

State Flag

Saguaro Cactus Blossom

Cactus Wren

The Grand Canyon

AR
Little Rock ★

ARKANSAS
The Natural State

Adam goes to Arkansas. What does he do?

Digs for diamonds

State Flag

Apple Blossom

Mockingbird

CALIFORNIA
The Golden State

Sacramento

CA

Charlene goes to California. What does she see?

State Flag

Golden Poppy

Valley Quail

The Golden Gate Bridge

COLORADO
The Centennial State

★ Denver

CO

Cameron goes to Colorado. What does he see?

Rocky Mountains

State Flag

Rocky Mountain Columbine

Lark Bunting

CONNECTICUT
The Constitution State

Hartford ★

CT

Caroline goes to Connecticut. What does she do?

State Flag

Mountain Laurel

Robin

Takes a lighthouse tour

DELAWARE
The First State

Dover ★ DE

Darcy goes to Delaware. What does she see?

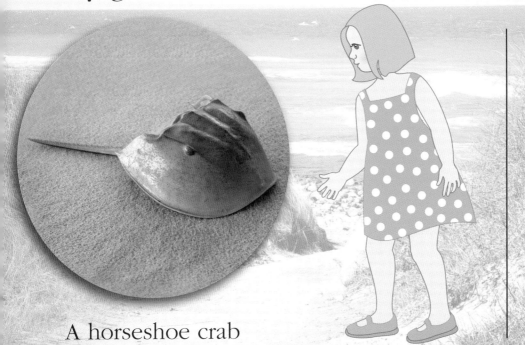

A horseshoe crab

State Flag

Peach Blossom

Blue Hen Chicken

FLORIDA
The Sunshine State

Tallahassee
FL

Felicia goes to Florida. Where does she visit?

State Flag

Orange Blossom

Mockingbird

Alligator Alley

GEORGIA
The Peach State

★ Atlanta

GA

Geraldo goes to Georgia. What does he do?

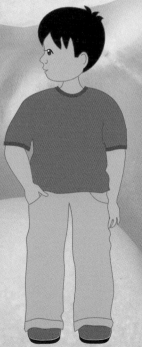

State Flag

Cherokee Rose

Brown Thrasher

Tours historic Savannah

Honolulu ★

HI

HAWAII
The Aloha State

Haley goes to Hawaii. Where does she visit?

State Flag

Hibiscus

Hawaiian Goose

Volcano National Park

IDAHO
The Gem State

Ian goes to Idaho. What does he do?

Visits a potato farm

State Flag

Syringa

Mountain Bluebird

Springfield

★

IL

ILLINOIS
The Prairie State

Irene goes to Illinois. What does she see?

State Flag

Purple Violet

Cardinal

Sears Tower

INDIANA
The Hoosier State

Ike goes to Indiana. What does he do?

Walks through corn fields

State Flag

Peony

Cardinal

IA
Des Moines ★

IOWA
The Hawkeye State

Indira goes to Iowa. What does she see?

State Flag

Wild Prairie Rose

Eastern Goldfinch

The Bridges of Madison Cour

KANSAS
The Sunflower State

KS Topeka ★

Kyle goes to Kansas. Where does he visit?

Wheat farm

State Flag

Sunflower

Western Meadowlark

KENTUCKY
The Bluegrass State

KY

★ Frankfort

Katrina goes to Kentucky. What does she do?

State Flag

Goldenrod

Cardinal

Rides horses

LOUISIANA
The Pelican State

Baton Rouge ★

Lolly goes to Louisiana. What does she see?

State Flag

Magnolia

Eastern Brown Pelican

owns at the Mardi Gras parade

MAINE
The Pine Tree State

ME

Augusta ★

Max goes to Maine. What does he do?

State Flag

White Pine Cone and Tassel

Chickadee

Canoes on the Allagash River

MARYLAND
The Old Line State

MD
Annapolis ★

Maggie goes to Maryland. Where does she visit?

Annapolis Harbor

State Flag

Black-eyed Susan

Baltimore Oriole

MASSACHUSETTS
The Bay State

MA · Boston ★

Michael goes to Massachusetts. Where does he visit

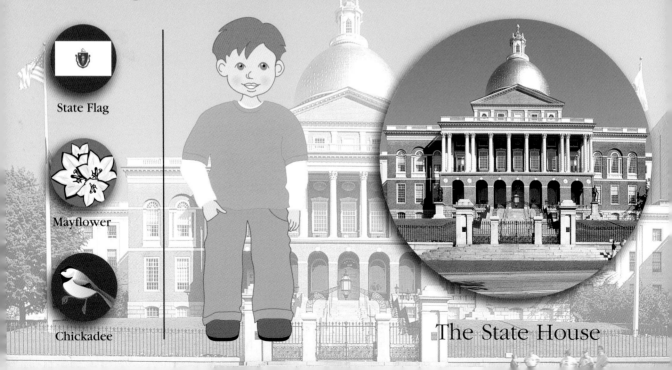

State Flag

Mayflower

Chickadee

The State House

MICHIGAN
The Wolverine State

MI
Lansing ★

Maurice goes to Michigan. What does he see?

Michigan Falls

State Flag

Apple Blossom

Robin

MINNESOTA
The North Star State

Meghan goes to Minnesota. What does she do?

State Flag

Pink and White Lady's Slipper

Loon

Ice fishing

Milo goes to Mississippi. What does he do?

State Flag

Magnolia

Mockingbird

Takes a steamboat ride

MISSOURI
The Show Me State

Jefferson City ★

MO

Mieko goes to Missouri. What does she see?

State Flag

Hawthorn

Bluebird

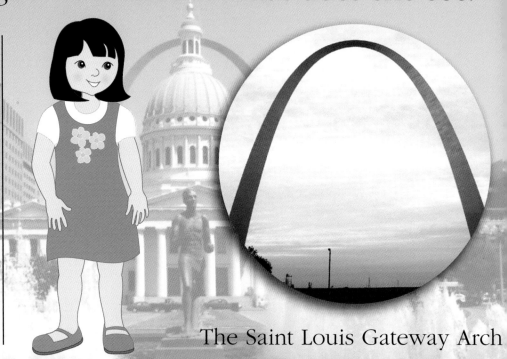

The Saint Louis Gateway Arch

MT
★ Helena

MONTANA
The Treasure State

Molly goes to Montana. What does she see?

American Bison

State Flag

Bitterroot

Western Meadowlark

NEBRASKA
The Cornhusker State

NE

Lincoln ★

Nick goes to Nebraska. What does he see?

State Flag

Goldenrod

Western Meadowlark

The Scotts Bluff National Monumen

NV
Carson

NEVADA
The Silver State

Natalie goes to Nevada. What does she see?

State Flag

Sagebrush

The Hoover Dam

Mountain Bluebird

NH Concord ★

NEW HAMPSHIRE
The Granite State

Nelson goes to New Hampshire. Where does he visi

State Flag

Purple Lilac

Purple Finch

Mount Washington

Nilda goes to New Jersey. Where does she go?

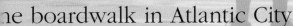
he boardwalk in Atlantic City

State Flag

Violet

Eastern Goldfinch

NEW MEXICO
The Land of Enchantment

Santa Fe ★

NM

Nina goes to New Mexico. Where does she visit:

State Flag

Yucca Flower

Roadrunner

Carlsbad Caverns

NEW YORK

The Empire State

NY Albany ★

Nathan goes to New York. What does he see?

The Statue of Liberty

State Flag

Rose

Bluebird

NORTH CAROLINA
The Tar Heel State

Raleigh ★ NC

Natasha goes to North Carolina. What does she see

State Flag

Dogwood

Cardinal

Green Turtles

Nikki goes to North Dakota. Where does she visit?

North Dakota Badlands

State Flag

Wild Prairie Rose

Western Meadowlark

OHIO
The Buckeye State

OH
Columbus ★

Oscar goes to Ohio. What does he see?

State Flag

Scarlet Carnation

Cardinal

The Cincinnati skyline

OKLAHOMA
The Sooner State

Oklahoma City ★ OK

Owen goes to Oklahoma. What does he see?

Oil pumpjack

State Flag

Mistletoe

Scissor-tailed Flycatcher

★ Salem

OR

OREGON
The Beaver State

Olivia goes to Oregon. What does she do?

State Flag

Oregon Grape

Western Meadowlark

Plays in the snow at Mount Hood

PENNSYLVANIA

PA

Harrisburg ★

The Keystone State

Patty goes to Pennsylvania. What does she see?

Liberty Bell

State Flag

Mountain Laurel

Ruffed Grouse

Providence ★

RHODE ISLAND
The Ocean State

RI

Robert goes to Rhode Island. What does he ride?

State Flag

Violet

Rhode Island Red

The Flying Horse Carousel

SOUTH CAROLINA
The Palmetto State

SC ★ Columbia

arah goes to South Carolina. Where does she visit?

Myrtle Beach

State Flag

Yellow Jessamine

Great Carolina Wren

Serafina goes to South Dakota. What does she se

State Flag

Pasque Flower

Ring-necked Pheasant

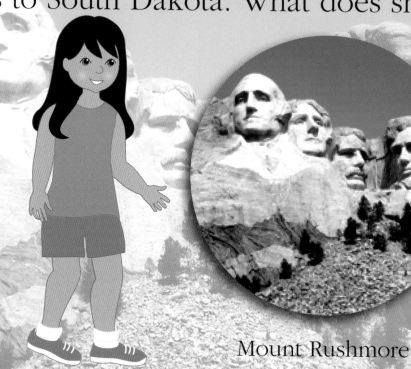

Mount Rushmore

TENNESSEE
The Volunteer State

Tanya goes to Tennessee. Where does she visit?

State Flag

Iris

Mockingbird

ecording studios in Nashville

TEXAS
The Lone Star State

Timmy goes to Texas. What does he see?

State Flag

Bluebonnet

Mockingbird

Cowboys at the rodeo

Ursula goes to Utah. What does she see?

The Mormon Tabernacle

State Flag

Sego lily

Seagull

Montpelier ★

VT

VERMONT
The Green Mountain State

Vincent goes to Vermont. What does he do?

State Flag

Red Clover

Hermit Thrush

Cross-country skiing

VIRGINIA
The Old Dominion State

VA
Richmond ★

Victoria goes to Virginia. What does she see?

State Flag

Dogwood

Cardinal

olonial buildings in Williamsburg

WASHINGTON
The Evergreen State

WA

★ Olympia

Winston goes to Washington. What does he see:

State Flag

Pink Rhododendron

Willow Goldfinch

Seattle's Space Needle

WEST VIRGINIA
The Mountain State

WV
★ Charleston

Warren goes to West Virginia. What does he see?

Blackwater Falls

State Flag

Rhododendron

Cardinal

WISCONSIN
The Badger State

Madison ★

Wendy goes to Wisconsin. What does she do?

State Flag

Wood Violet

Robin

Visits Lake Superior Basin

WY

WYOMING
The Equality State

Cheyenne ★

Wyatt goes to Wyoming. What does he see?

Old Faithful Geyser

State Flag

Indian Paintbrush

Western Meadowlark

Sorella

www.sorellabooks.com